THE GOLDEN TOUCH

Faith, Family, and Friends

A COLLECTION
OF FAVORITE RECIPES

VJ PUBLISHING HOUSE, LLC.
20451 NW 2ND AVENUE. SUITE 112
MIAMI GARDENS, FLORIDA 33169

www.vjpublishinghouse.com

@2021 vjpublishinghouse, llc. All rights reserved.

06/27/2021
ISBN: 978-1-939236-11-1

Printed in the United States of America

IN MEMORY OF OUR "DAISY"

Few people realize their life's mission before departing this earth. However, the best testimony to one's experience is the "LOVE" of those left behind. So is the legacy of Daisy Bell Golden.

Her desire to share with others spiritual food (the word of God) and physical food (seven-layer cakes, egg pies, butter rolls, and her famous teacakes) was a testament to being an "Earthly Angel." Although absent from our presence, she continues to impact our lives as evidence of these favorite recipes in this
"The Golden Touch Cookbook!"

A HEAP OF GOOD OLE' RECIPES! ENJOY!!!

AUNTY ROE'S AMAZING ANGEL EGGS

Ingredients:
One dozen large eggs
2 Tablespoons of Relish (sweet or dill)
½ Tablespoon of Mustard
1 1/2 Tablespoons of Mayonnaise
2 Pinches of Accent
1 Pinch of Salt
½ teaspoon of Onion Powder
1 Pinch of Red crushed Peppers
1 Pinch of White Pepper
1 Tablespoon of Sugar
½ Teaspoon of Olive Oil
1 Pinch of Paprika

DIRECTIONS

Boil eggs in water and ½ Teaspoon of Olive Oil until they are hard
Allow eggs to cool or settle them in cold water
Once eggs are cool, peel and soak in water to remove any shell pieces
Gently slice the eggs in halves removing the yoke and place aside;
Place eggs in clean water to remove excess, rinse and place eggs in the refrigerator for 5-10 minutes to dry
Mash yolk in a bowl until delicate and smooth
Mix Mayo, Mustard, Relish with Yolk
Add Crushed Pepper, White Pepper, Onion Powder, Accent, Salt, and Sugar to mixture
Mix well together briskly Scoop teaspoon of yolk mixture and place in egg half
Sprinkle a pinch of Paprika on Top of Angel Egg & Serve

MORGHAN'S DOUBLE-DIP SCALLOP CHIPS

Ingredients:
½ Pound of fresh Scallops
Parsley
Oregano
Garlic Powder
Onion Powder
Lemon Pepper
Buttermilk
All-Purpose Flour
Vegetable Oil
Lemon Butter or Cocktail Sauce

DIRECTIONS

Put vegetable oil in a pot, pan, or deep fryer to heat

Clean, cut, and season Scallops to liking

Place scallops in a bowl and pour buttermilk to cover them fully

Allow scallops to sit in the mixture for 5-7 minutes

Pour flour into a brown paper bag and add scallops

Shake scallops in bag thoroughly

Shake off excess flour from each scallop

Dip scallops twice in buttermilk

Place scallops back into flour to prepare for frying

Drop each scallop into hot oil and fry to crispy brown at times
turning them

Remove from fryer and sit on paper towels to soak up excess oil

Enjoy with lemon butter sauce or cocktail sauce

TRACI'S WORLD-FAMOUS MEATBALLS

Ingredients:
Turkey or Beef Meat Balls
Heinz Chili sauce
16 oz. Welches Grape Jelly

DIRECTIONS

Preheat Oven to 350 degrees
Place Meatballs on Pan
Mix Chili Sauce and Grape Jelly together on the stovetop (Medium Heat) stir until it becomes of a liquid texture in a sauce-pan
Reduce heat to low and allow the sauce to sit for 5 minutes
Place meatballs in the oven and let them brown for 20-30 minutes
Place meatballs in colander to drain excess oil
Return meatballs to pan and pour mixture over meatballs
Place back into the oven for 15-20 minutes to give a glazed look Serve!

DANIELLE'S DELIGHTFUL ROTEL DIP

Ingredients:
10 ounce can of Rotel with green chili (mild or hot)
A pound of grass-fed ground beef
Pack Organic Sage 0.66 oz
8 Ounce Packs of Cream Cheese
4 Ounces of Sour Cream
Pepper
Salt
Garlic Powder
Onion Powder
BadiaSazon Complete Seasoning
Red Pepper Flakes
Lemon Pepper Seasoning
Tortilla Chips

Optional:
1 Tablespoon Minced Garlic
Half of a Diced White Onions
Pickled Jalapeños or Banana Pepper

DIRECTIONS

Allow cream cheese to reach room temperature before beginning
- Brown ground beef on medium heat in a deep-fry pan or sauce-pan
- Season ground beef to taste preferences (add optional onions and garlic)
- Finely mince sage (half of the pack or to your desired taste) add to ground beef while the meat is cooking
- Drain fat from ground beef
- Drain water from Rotel
- Add Rotel to ground beef in the pan
- Cut each package of cream cheese into eight blocks and add blocks slowly and even throughout the pan and stir into a smooth consistency over medium heat
- Add sour cream and continue to stir over medium heat until consistency is homogenously smooth
- If needed, add additional seasonings to the combination after all ingredients are combined and allow to simmer for 3-5 minutes while stirring
- Serve with tortilla chips
- Jalapeños or banana peppers can be added for extra flavor and spice before serving

VICTORIA'S CARRIBEAN CONCH SALAD

Ingredients:

1 lb. Conch
Red or Green Tomatoes
Onions
Scotch Bonnet Pepper
Salt
Cayenne Pepper
Onion Powder
Garlic Powder
Accent
Paprika
Complete seasoning
Crystal Hot Sauce
Lemons
Tablespoon White Vinegar

DIRECTIONS

Dice (untenderized) Conch into small chunks
Dice onions, tomatoes, and scotch bonnet into small pieces
Combine conch, tomatoes, onions, and scotch bonnet
together in a bowl with vinegar. Sprinkle salt, cayenne
pepper, onion powder, garlic powder, accent, and complete
seasoning into the mixture
Squeeze lemons into the salad to taste. Sprinkle a little more
accent for flavoring. Stir ingredients and serve!

Add Hot Sauce to your liking. ENJOY!!!

CAROLYN'S SIMPLY DELICIOUS CRABMEAT SPREAD!

Ingredients:
½ lb. of lump crabmeat
1 tablespoon of mayonnaise
1 teaspoon of lemon juice
1 teaspoon of Dijon Mustard
2 teaspoon of minced parsley
½ teaspoon of salt
¼ teaspoon cayenne pepper
6 whole chives blended

DIRECTIONS
Gently mix all ingredients and serve
on top of lettuce,small snack bread,
or cracker. Enjoy!!!

SHIRLEY'S SHRIMP HORS D'OEUVRES

Ingredients:
1 lb. fresh shrimp, cleaned and cooked
1 teaspoon minced onion
1 teaspoon minced celery
1 teaspoon chopped green pepper
2 teaspoon lemon juice
½ teaspoon grated lemon rind
1//4 teaspoon salt
4-5 drops of Tabasco sauce
Dash of pepper
¼ cup of mayonnaise
Crackers
Fresh parsley

DIRECTIONS
Cut shrimp into very fine pieces Combine all ingredients except
crackers and parsley Pile a heaping teaspoon of shrimp mix on each
cracker Garnish with parsley

REGINA'S CARRIBEAN SHRIMP COCKTAIL

Ingredients:

1 lb. peeled shrimp any size (deveined)
2Twoteaspoons Soy Sauce
1 cup red or white onions (finely chopped two
2 cloves of garlic (chopped)
1/2 cup ketchup
1/2 mayo
1/4 cup fresh cilantro chopped
1 1/2 cup lime juice

DIRECTIONS

In a bowl, marinate defrosted shrimp in 1 cup of lime juice for 5 minutes
Reserve the other half cup for later
In a frying pan, lightly brown the chopped garlic in a teaspoon of cooking oil. Set aside to cool down
Then in a bowl, combine the shrimp, the rest of lime juice, garlic, onions, cilantro, mayonnaise, soy sauce, and ketchup
Drain the shrimp. Add salt and pepper to taste. Mix up well

You can scoop up the cocktail with saltine crackers or fried green plantains

SELENA'S SWEET AND SOUR TURKEY BALLS

Ingredients:

1 lb. ground turkey
½ cup Italian bread crumbs
1 egg
1 cup ketchup
2 teaspoons cider vinegar
¼ cup brown sugar

Optional Sauce:
8-ounce can pineapple chunks with juice
Green peppers, chopped
Red peppers, chopped
Mushrooms, sliced

DIRECTIONS
Combine turkey, bread crumbs, and egg
Form into 1' balls and place on cookie sheet
Bake at 350-degrees for 20-30 minutes
In a large sauce-pan combine vinegar and brown sugar. (add pineapple chunks, peppers, and mushrooms, if desired)
Bring to a boil
Pour over turkey-balls and serve!

MEAT & POULTRY

ZACK'S ZESTY OLD SKOOL BURGERS!

Ingredients:

Ground Beef or Turkey
Hidden Valley Ranch Salad Dressing
Pinch of salt & pepper
Mayonnaise
Bell Peppers
Onions

DIRECTIONS

Mix all ingredients Separate into single amounts
size of the preferred burger Place burgers on
grill or oven and cook flipping at times
Remove burger upon the preference of liking
Serve on bun

GG'S Every-Ting Fiery Jerk Barbecue Turkey Wings"

Ingredients:

Oxtail seasoning
Jamaican Jerk seasoning
Black pepper
Onion powder
Pinch of Lawry's (not too much)
Two packs of onion gravy
Coconut Oil
Jamaican Jerk Barbecue Sauce
Sweet Baby Ray's BBQ Sauce.

DIRECTIONS

Season turkey wings to your liking with the above ingredients
Add a little less than a 1/2 cup of water to the crockpot, just enough for the turkey wings to make their juice and enough not to burn
Allow turkey wings to cook all the way through. Cover and cook on
high heat
Cut up potatoes, carrots, and season to your liking w/ likewise ingredients
Add butter beans if you like to your carrots and potatoes.
Once you have allowed your meat to cook through, add your carrots and potatoes; cover and cook on high heat.
In a bowl, add jerk sauces, seasoning, and BBQ sauce in one bowl.
Add a little honey and a little water to loosen the sauce and mix
Allow potatoes to cook through a little but not too soft before adding sauce
Lastly, add sauce, cover, and cook on medium heat
Cook until your liking. Taste for flavor as you go

VALERIE'S SOUTHERN "GIRL" PORK SOUSE!

Ingredients:

Pork Meat (Pig feet, Pig Ears, Hog Maw) All Chopped into pieces
White Vinegar
Lemon Juice
Salt
White Pepper
Accent
All Spice
Crushed Red Pepper
Onion Powder
Garlic Powder
Complete Seasoning
Limes

DIRECTIONS

Wash Pork Meat thoroughly
Place Meat into Pot and Boil for 8 minutes
Rinse/clean meat thoroughly & remove excess from Meat and Pot
Place back in pot and boil meat again for 8 minutes
Rinse/clean Pork thoroughly again & remove excess
Final, rewash Meat and place in a clean pot with water covering the meat. Pour 1/4 cup of vinegar into Pot with Meat covered by water
Stir in bay leaves, All Spice, Onion Powder, Garlic Powder, Salt, White Pepper, & Complete Seasoning. Stir and Boil for 45-60 minutes on Medium High Setting
Add Accent, Crushed Pepper, Lemon Juice boiling for 15-20 more minutes. Remove from heat and taste for flavoring
Add extra seasoning if needed
Serve with hot sauce and fresh lime sprinkled on meat

SOMIA'S NECK BONES

Ingredients:

5lbs. pork neckbones chopped up
1 large chopped onions
Salt/pepper
Flour
Water

DIRECTIONS

Clean meat
Place meat in pot cover with water
Add onion, salt and pepper
Cover and cook medium heat
In a cup mix 2 tablespoons of flour with
water and add to pot as a thickener

CONCHITA'S CHICKEN & RAISIN'S DISH

Ingredients:

1) Chicken Pieces
2) Seasonings to your desire.
3) 1 onion
4) 3/4 stick of butter or margarine
5) olive oil
6) 1 box of Sun-Maid raisins

DIRECTIONS

Clean chicken as you usually do Season chicken thoroughly
In a skillet large enough to accommodate chicken pieces, coat bottom with
olive oil (enough to brown the chicken) Once the chicken is browned, add
butter/margarine Cut onion into slices & add to chicken and cook until
onion is almost sautéed Add raisins according to pieces of chicken If using
a whole chicken, use half, the box of raisins If using smaller portions, only
use a small portion of raisins Let simmer until chicken, onions & raisins are
done
This dish goes very well over a plate of white rice or whatever rice you like
Enjoy & Bon-appetite

KISHAMMEE'S CHICKEN PURLO & RICE

Ingredients:

Chicken (any desired part)
Stick of margarine Salt and pepper
1 chopped onion Rice Yellow food
coloring Water

DIRECTIONS

Clean chicken Place in pot with
water
Add salt/ pepper/onion and 1 small
cap
of yellow food coloring Let chicken
cook until ½ done Add desired
amount of rice to mixture Stir and
place lid on top Cook on medium
low until done stir occasionally

DANIELLE'S GROUND TURKEY STUFFED PEPPERS

Ingredients:

• Five medium green, red or yellow bell peppers
• Two teaspoons olive oil
• Cooking spray
• 1-1/4 pounds extra-lean ground turkey (99% lean)
• One large onion, chopped
• One garlic clove, mince two teaspoons ground cumin
• One teaspoon Italian seasoning
• 1/2 teaspoon salt
• 1/2 teaspoon pepper
• 2 cups shredded extra-sharp cheddar cheese
• 1/4 teaspoon paprika
• 8 Ounce Tomato Paste

DIRECTIONS

* 1. Preheat oven to 375
* 2. Cut peppers lengthwise in half; remove seeds and inside
* 3. Line a glass baking dish with foil
* 4. Coat foil with cooking spray
* 5. Pour olive oil in a pan and brown the ground turkey on medium-high,and add seasonings
* 6. Add onion and garlic and continue to cook
* 7. Add tomato paste and stir in ¼ to ½ cup of water; add additional seasoning if necessary, for taste
* 8. Add rice slowly and stir into a consistent mixture (optional)
* 9. Fill bell pepper halves with the mixture using a spoon and place peppers into a baking dish with the mixture facing upward Top with sharp cheddar cheese and bake until cheese is melted, remove promptly when cheese begins to brown, and Garnish with parmesan cheese and cilantro

QUAY'S SPECIALTY TACO'S

Ingredients:

Olive Oil for frying tortillas
Corn Tortilla
Ground beef 90% to 93% lean
Refried Beans
Taco Topping:
Shredded cheese
Shredded lettuce
Chopped tomatoes
Diced onion
Sliced avocado
Sour cream
Guacamole

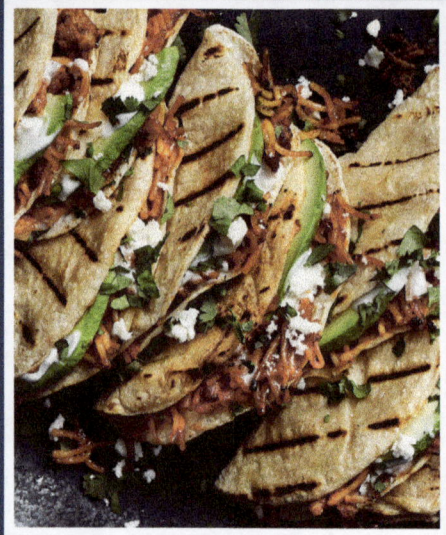

Making The Taco Shells

Heat about 1 inch of oil in a heavy skillet over medium to medium-high heat to 365 degrees F (180 degrees C).
Use tongs to place one tortilla at a time into the oil. It should start to sizzle right away. Cook for about 15 seconds, then flip over and fold the shell in half, holding in place with the tongs until crispy, about 15 seconds. You may need a little practice at first. Drain on paper towels, and sprinkle with salt while still hot. Use for tacos right away, or they may become chewy. Leftovers may be heated in the oven for crisping

Making The Ground Beef

Heat 1 Tbsp olive oil in a 12-inch non-stick skillet over medium-high heat.Add beef to skillet and season with salt and pepper.
Let brown on bottom, about 3 minutes then flip, break up beef and continue to sear until almost cooked through, about 2 minutes.
Add garlic, chili powder, cumin, onion powder and cook until just cooked through, about 1 minute
Pour in chicken broth and tomato sauce.
Simmer over medium-low heat until sauce has reduced and thickened, about 3 – 5 minutes.Serve taco filling warm over warmed tortillas with the desired toppings of your choice. ENJOY!

MARINA'S GOOD, GOOD! GRIOT

Ingredients:

5lbs of pork
shoulder (cut into small chunks)
3 limes
1 sour orange
Epis seasoning
Complete seasoning
Adobo seasoning
1 chicken Maggie
Thyme
Scotch bonnet pepper
Onions and bell peppers (optional)

DIRECTIONS

- squeeze lime juice into a bowl
- use lime skin and hot water to wash meat
- place cleaned meat in a bowl
- pour the lime juice and sour orange over the meat
- add seasonings to liking mix well
- add meat, thyme, and scotch bonnet in a pot bring to a boil
- lower to medium heat
- cook for 20-30 minutes on low-medium heat
- fry to golden brown or preferred liking
- slice onions and bell peppers for garnish

BIANCA'S GRILLED LAMB CHOPS

Ingredients:

2 large lemons
¼ cup olive oil 2 to 3 cloves garlic
2 tablespoons fresh oregano leaves, finely
chopped (or dry if that's what you have)
1 teaspoon fresh thyme leaves, roughly chopped
1 whole bay leaf
1 teaspoons of salt of your choice (to your taste)
Fresh parsley (handful less than a bunch)
1 tablespoon of fresh Rosemary
Cayenne pepper (to your taste)
1 teaspoon of black pepper

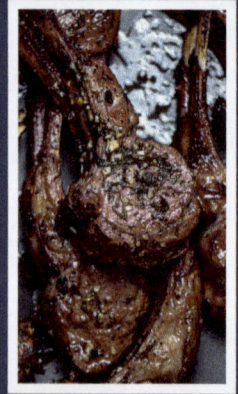

DIRECTIONS

Rough Blend or use food processor all ingredients. Add more lemon
juice or oil if needed. Marinade 4-24 hours.
Grill 3 minutes each side for medium done and serve!

LUCY'S BROCCOLI AND CHICKEN CASSEROLE

Ingredients:

8 Chicken Thighs (substitute
chicken breast if you prefer)
4 Cups Uncle Bens Rice
8 cups water (seasoned chicken
broth)
2 Bags Frozen Broccoli
Velveeta Cheese (8 to 12 oz.)
Cream Cheese (8 oz.)

Shredded Mix Cheeses (16 oz.)
Onion (1 large)
Bell pepper (1 large)
Mushrooms (optional)
1 Small Can French's Fried Onions
(optional)
Seasonings to taste

DIRECTIONS

Boil chicken parts with seasonings. Make rice, use water or chicken broth.
Debone chicken, mix with rice, sautéed veggies, broccoli, velveeta cheese
& cream cheese in a large tin pan or casserole dish. Sprinkle shredded mix
cheese on top bake on 400-degrees for approximately 30 minutes. Top
with canned fried onions for the last 10 minutes

ABBY'S AMAZING FIERY FRIED TURKEY WINGS!!!

Ingredients:

Turkey Wings (Have each section cut into three pieces)
Lemon Juice
Sour Orange
Chicken Bouillon Cubes
Goya Adobo Seasoning (Blue Top)
Lawry's Seasoning
Lemon Pepper
Accent
Onion Powder
Cayenne Pepper
Vegetable Oil

DIRECTIONS

Wash Turkey wings thoroughly
Boil in water on high heat for 20 minutes
Pour water off and rinse again
Boil again with lemon juice, sour orange, and a couple
of chicken cubes for 45 minutes
Pour water off and allow them to sit for 30 minutes to dry
Season with Goya. Seasoning
Shake Lawry's Season Salt, Lemon Pepper, Accent, Complete Seasoning,
and Onion Powder
Add Cayenne Pepper if you prefer Spicey
Allow all ingredients to Marinade for 1 hour
Make sure pot/fry pan is hot with oil
Drop meat in the pot/fry pan one piece at a time
Cover with a top so that the oil doesn't pop out
Fry for 20 minutes, continuously flipping meat so it can brown
Remove and place on paper towel to drain excess oil

VERONICA'S FINGER LICKING SHORT RIBS!

- Carrots
- Celery
- 1 Fennel (or scallion)
- Shitake Mushrooms
- 1 Jalapeno diced
- 1 leak
- 1 Onion diced
- Kosher Salt
- Short Ribs
- Black Pepper
- Flour
- Garlic cloves minced
- Bay leaves
- Tomato paste, 2 tablespoons
- Vegetable oil
- Butter, 2 tablespoons
- Olive oil, 2 tablespoons
- Red wine (good wine)
- Bundle of herbs (thyme, Rosemary, etc.)
- Herbs de Provence
- Onion Powder
- Beef stock

DIRECTIONS

Use a heavy pot. I suggest a Dutch pot or cast iron.

Preheat oven to 300 degrees. Remove short ribs from the fridge and allow them to come to room temperature. Season with kosher salt and pepper

Sprinkle with flour or dredge the meat through the flour.Heat pot with vegetable oil. When the oil is heated (you'll see light whisps of smoke), sear the short ribs on each side until browned. You may have to do this in batches, so please don't overcrowd the Dutch oven; otherwise, they'll steam instead of brown. Browning can take up to 15 minutes, depending on how many short ribs you have. Transfer browned short ribs to a plate and set aside

Add 2 tablespoons of olive oil plus 2 tablespoons of butter, and scrape up the browned bits using a wooden spoon or rubber spatula. When the butter is melted, add all the vegetables. They should be diced. Sauté all the vegetables and season with salt and pepper. Sauté until softened. Add in minced garlic and tomato paste and sauté some more, about 2-5 mins. Then pour in ¾ cup of the red wine. Immediately scrape up any browned bits at the bottom of the pan and allow the wine to cook down for about a minute or two. The better the wine, the better the flavor!!!

Now place the bundle of herbs in the pot. If you don't have a pile of fresh herbs, you can use dry herbs (Rosemary, thyme, etc.). Place the short ribs back in the pot and add the beef stock (you can add chicken stock if you don't have enough of the beef) now, bring to a boil.Once the pot comes to a boil, cover and place the Dutch Pot in the oven should be heated to 300 degrees—Bake for 4 hours. After 4 hours, remove the short ribs from the oven. Meat should be tender and falling off the bone. If for brunch, serve over grits. Dinner, over rice. I hope you enjoy it!

JOANNA'S CHICKEN GUMBO WITH ANDOUILLE SAUSAGE

Ingredients:
1cup veg oil
1cup flour
1 large onion
1 large bell pepper
3 stalks celery
4 cloves garlic
1 bunch green onion
1 lb. andouille sausage
4 chicken breasts
1 bloc chicken stock
2 cups of water
Bay leaf, cayenne, salt/pepper, & Seafood Seasoning

DIRECTIONS

Add flour and oil to a large pot (be sure it has a tight-fitting lid) cook until chocolate color dark but not burned, about 30-40 minutes constantly stirring
Add veggies (only white part of green onions), sausage, and seasonings
Cook, stirring for several minutes, until vegetables are wilt
Add chicken stock and water
Add chicken and cook for 45 minutes, covered
Remove chicken shred, and return to pot
Simmer for 45min-1 hour more
Add green onions and serve over rice

VAL'S PEPPER STEAK

Ingredients:
1 1/2 lb. steak (cut in strips)
3 green peppers, diced
1 large onion, chopped
1 tablespoon Soy Sauce
1 tablespoon of all-purpose flour
Vegetable oil
1 teaspoon of Worcestershire Sauce
¼ cup of water
Dash of Accent
Salt to taste
Pepper to taste

DIRECTIONS

Place meat in a skillet with vegetable oil and simmer
In a separate pan, add vegetable oil with flour and stir until browned
Add water to make the sauce, adding onions, peppers, and remaining ingredients, stirring gently. Pour mixture over steak in skillet and allow to simmer on low heat. Taste to liking

WAYNE'S TERIYAKI CHICKEN WINGS!

Ingredients:
1 lb. Chicken Wings
1 teaspoon of ground ginger
1 garlic clove, minced
½ cup of soy sauce
¼ cup of sherry
1 teaspoon of sugar

DIRECTIONS

Cut cleaned wings into pieces at the joint and place them in a single
Layer in a shallow roasting pan
Roast uncovered at 375 degrees for 30 minutes or until skin is crisp
Combine remaining ingredients and pour over chicken wings
Smear sauce to cover all wing pieces
Cover pan tightly with foil and bake another 30 minutes or until wings are browned and tender but not dry

LISA'S LEMON BARBECUED CHICKEN

Ingredients:
1 ½ lb. skinless, boneless chicken breast
Dash of Pa▢prika
Dash of Cayenne Pepper
3 tablespoon lemon juice
1 tablespoon of honey

DIRECTIONS

Season cleaned chicken with paprika and pepper
Combine lemon juice and honey and set 2 tablespoons aside
Place chicken on broiler rack or charcoal grill
Broil for 15 minutes, occasionally basting with lemon honey mixture
turning chicken over basting with honey mixture and broil for 15 additional minutes.
Spoon sauce over chicken just before serving

SEAFOOD

SHANNON'S HONEY BARBECUE GLAZED SALMON

Ingredients:

Salmon Fillets
1/2 Cup of BBQ Sauce
1/3 Cup of a honey teaspoon of
diced Ginger
2 Diced Garlic Cloves

DIRECTIONS

Preheat Oven to 350 degrees
Place Salmon on Baking Sheet or Pan
Cover with foil and bake for 20 minutes
Whisk BBQ Sauce, Honey, Garlic & Ginger
Spread Sauce on top of each fillet
Return Salmon to Oven without foil for 5-7 minutes
Remove from oven allow to cool and serve

DONNA'S BROWN STEW FISH DISH

Ingredients:

Fish (Red Snapper/Grouper/Yellow Tail)
Lemon Juice/Lime Juice
Grace Jerk Sauce
Adobe All Purpose Seasoning
Black Pepper
Olive Oil
Vegetable Oil
Carrots
Onions
Bell Pepper

Directions:

Wash fish in lime/lemon water
Season fish with port royal fish fry
Add a little Grace Jerk Sauce and all-purpose seasoning, and black pepper
Also, brush Jerk sauce inside the fish and allow it to sit for 30-45 minutes
Heat frypan on High, then pour either olive or vegetable oil into a pan
Place the fish into to fry pan, and when it's golden brown on one side, you flip it. Cut up veggies that you wish to used (i.e., carrots,onions, bell pepper)
Add 1 cup water and season to taste
Bring to a full boil, then add fish simmer for 5-10 min then serve

FELICE'S DOREEN'S STYLE BOIL FISH

Ingredients;

1 medium grouper head
2 onions
1 bunch of green onions
½ pack bay leave
1 stick of butter
Nature season's seasonings
Salt/Pepper
Accent
Lemon Juice

Directions:

Season your grouper head with salt, pepper, nature seasoning and accentin a Medium boiling pot. Saturate butter, bay leaves, chopped onions/green onions also. Simmer for 5minutes, then add grouper head. it cook slow for about 30 minutes. Add lemon juice to taste preference. Serve!!!!

LALAR'S AWESOME ESCOVITCH FISH !

Ingredients:

- Red Snapper or Yellow Tail
- Accent
- Season salt
- Complete seasoning
- Onion powder
- Garlic powder
- Lemon pepper
- Vegetable oil
- Onion
- Thyme
- Green pepper
- Yellow pepper
- Orange pepper
- White vinegar
- Soy sauce
- Browning sauce
- Scotch bonnet or red pepper (optional)

Directions:

Dry fish with paper towels. Slice fish on each side. Mix all the seasonings and sprinkle on each side of fish

Use a big frying pan and heat oil—Fry fish brown on both sides. (fry fish hard). Place fried fish in a long pan. Dice onions and peppers

Pour the oil out of the pan. Leave a little oil in the pan and sauté the onions and peppers together. Pour white vinegar into the pan, just enough to cover the onions and pepper. Add soy sauce and a little browning sauce into the pan. Mix more seasoning and add scotch bonnet or red pepper if you want more spice. Pour mixture over fried fish in the long pan and let sit for 10 mins. Ready to eat!!

GAIL SEAY'S SAUCY SHRIMP & GRITS!

Ingredients:

1 pound of fresh shrimp
1 red bell pepper
1 yellow bell pepper
1 green bell pepper
1 large sweet option
2 sticks of butter
Creole Seasoning
Chicken Bouillon
Sea Salt
Garlic Salt
Oh! Bay Seasoning

Directions:

Cut Veggies in small vertical slices and Sautee them in butter on medium and add seasoning to taste.
Clean fresh shrimp and dry them off. Add seasonings lightly to shrimp. After veggie s are soft, add shrimp for 6 to 8 minutes.
Grits: add cream cheese, butter, and carnation milk to 5 min grits in the box

VALENCIA'S CREAMY SHRIMP PASTA DISH

Ingredients:
Chopped green onion
Minced garlic
Parsley
Paprika
Garlic powder
Onion powder
Old bay
Black pepper
Red crush pepper
Accent
Butter
Heavy whipping cream
Parmesan Cheese
Asiago cheese
Boil fettuccine noodles for 10-12 minutes

Directions:
Season shrimp and green onion with seasonings above
Low heat melt butter, add minced garlic, pour heavy cream, and whisk slowly
Add Parmesan and Asiago cheese whisk slowly until a thickened consistency is formed
Add noodles and cooked shrimp to the Alfredo sauce and mix
Sprinkle parsley (optional)

CARL'S CRAZY CRAB CAKES!

Ingredients;
1 lb. Crabmeat
1 egg, slightly beaten
½ cup of bread crumbs
1 tablespoon of finely chopped green pepper
1 tablespoon of chopped onion
¼ cup mayonnaise
1 tablespoon of mustard
1 tablespoon of lemon juice
Salt & pepper to taste
Butter or margarine

Directions:
Slightly flake crabmeat
Add remaining ingredients
Form and pat into round cakes
In a skillet, add butter or margarine and fry crab cakes
Flipping until golden brown.
Serve!

PERRIE'S BAKED OYSTERS ITALIAN STYLE

Ingredients:
½ cup of olive oil
2 bunches of scallions, top and bottom finely chopped
1 ¼ cup of cracker crumbs
¼ cup of grated parmesan cheese
½ teaspoon of salt
1 quart of oysters drained and patted dry

Directions:
Coat bottom of baking dish with a thin layer of oil
Combine onions, cracker crumbs, cheese, and salt
Generously sprinkle a portion over the bottom of the pan
Place layer of oysters over crackers
Sprinkle with crumbs mixture
Repeat until oysters and crumbs are used up
ending with crumbs on top
Stream olive oil over the entire top layer
Bake at 375-degrees for 45 minutes or until juices
are thickened and golden brown

LARRY'S CRAZY CRAB BOIL

Ingredients:
A few tablespoons of seafood seasoning (i.e., Old Bay)
3 lbs. of cut potatoes
2 16 oz. packages of cooked kielbasa sausages (cut
   into 1-inch pieces
8 ears of shucked corn cut into thirds
4 lbs. of frozen crab legs

Directions:
Heat a large pot of water over medium-high heat indoors or outside. Add
the seafood seasoning to taste and bring to a boil
Add the potatoes and sausage and cook until the potatoes are fork-tender,
about 10 minutes. Add the corn and cook
for about five more minutes. Add the crab and cook another 5 minutes.
Add the shrimp and cook until they turn pink, another 3 or 4 minutes

CASSEROLES &VEGGIE DISHES

THE KOUNTIST TUNA CASSEROLE

Ingredients:
½ boxes of Shell noodles
Shredded cheddar cheese
2-4 cans of tuna
One can Cream of mushroom
One can Cream of broccoli
1 can Cream of celery soup
1-of 2 cans water
Salt and pepper to taste

Directions:
Boil noodles
Drain and rinse
Mix all ingredients
Bake for 20-30 minutes

ROZZ'S CREAMY MACARONI CHEESY CHEESE!
Ingredients:

36 oz. Box of Muller's Elbow Macaroni
4 Large Eggs
Two cans of carnation evaporated milk
One stick of butter
One bar of Country Crock
1 16 oz. Bag (1lb. Cheddar or Mild Cheese)
1 10 oz. Bag (1 lb. Sharp Cheddar Cheese)
Add more cheese to liking (optional). However,
if you add more cheese, you need more milk
One can of Cream of Mushroom Soup
One small container of Sour Cream

Directions:

Combine the above ingredients and add Salt, Black Pepper, and Accent to taste
Stir all ingredients well and smooth into a layer
Bake in a 350-degree oven for 45 minutes. Serve!

CARLEETHA'S COME BACK FOR MORE CORN PUDDING!!!

Ingredients:
One box of Jiffy Corn Bread Mix
One can of cream-style corn
One can of whole kernel corn
8 ounces of sour cream
One stick of margarine
1 cup whole milk
1/2 cup white sugar
Two eggs.

Directions:
Pre-heat Oven 350 degrees
In a bowl, pour both cans of corn and Jiffy mix, stir well
Add milk, sugar, sour cream, and eggs. Mix well
Slice up margarine and add to mixture
Pour into baking pan and let bake for 20 minutes and stir
Continue baking until done
Stick a toothpick in the center of the pudding. If it comes out clean, it's ready

KIMMY'S CANDIED YAMS

Ingredients:

2 lbs. fresh yams, peeled and sliced ¼ inch
1 cup of water
1 teaspoon of vanilla extract
4 tablespoon (1/2 stick) unsalted butter softened
½ cup of granulated sugar
½ cup of brown sugar
½ teaspoon of ground cinnamon
½ teaspoon of allspice
2 cups of pineapple chunks

Directions:

Place yams in greased baking pan
Combine water and vanilla and pour over yams
Combine butter, sugars, cinnamon, and allspice
Sprinkle over yams
Cover pan tightly and bake at 400-degrees for 45 minutes
Sprinkle pineapple over yams
Baste with juices in the pan
Cover and continue baking for about 20 minutes or until
yams are tender, and juices are bubbling
Serve hot

CATHERINE'S FRIED GREEN TOMATOES

Ingredients:

2 large unpeeled tomatoes
1 egg beaten with one tablespoon of water
½ cup of lightly salted dry-bread crumbs
3 tablespoons of bacon fat or vegetable oil

Directions:

Cut tomatoes into ¼ thick slices
Dip slices into egg-water mixture and coat
with bread crumbs
Fry slices in medium heat hot oil until golden brown
on both sides and tender throughout
Drain on paper towels. Serve!

JACKIE'S SOUTHERN COOKED RUTABAGAS

Ingredients:

2 lbs. of rutabaga, peeled and cubed
3 cups of water
¼ pound of salt pork, rinsed and sliced
1 teaspoon of sugar
½ teaspoon of salt
¼ teaspoon of pepper, plus additional pepper to taste

Directions:

Combine rutabaga, water, salt pork, sugar, and salt in
Large sauce-pan. Bring to a boil. Reduce heat and simmer
Uncovered for 35 minutes or until rutabaga is tender
Drain, remove and discard salt pork
Add ¼ teaspoon pepper to rutabaga and mash to desired consistency. Sprinkle with additional pepper

JOANNE'S COLLARD GREENS WITH HAM HOCKS

Ingredients:

1 smoked ham hock
4 cups of water
2 lbs. of collard greens
1 teaspoon of salt
1 ½ teaspoon of crushed red pepper flakes
1 tablespoon of salt
¼ cup of bacon drippings

Directions:

Place ham hock in a 5-quart pot with water
Cover and bring to boil
Reduce heat and simmer for 45 minutes
Skim foam from broth several times
Cut and remove thick part of collard stems and wash thoroughly
Drain greens, chop into small pieces adding to ham hock and broth
Stir in salt, red pepper, sugar, and bacon drippings
Cover and cook at medium-low heat for 20 minutes or
until greens are tender
Turn off heat and allow to sit for 10 minutes before serving
Optional: Instead of ham hock, you can substitute with turkey
Serve hot

LINDA'S STIR-FRY CABBAGE

Ingredients:

2 strips of bacon, cut into squares
½ cup of onions
½ cup of chopped green peppers
1 firm head white cabbage
¼ teaspoon garlic powder
¼ teaspoon black pepper, according to taste preference
¼ teaspoon five-spice powder, according to
taste preference
½ cup of water
2 tablespoons of soy sauce.

Directions:

Cook bacon in Dutch oven until soft and stir in onions
and green peppers, sauté' until clear
Cut up cabbage coarsely, rinse and drain
Add to Dutch oven, mix well
Sprinkle with garlic powder, pepper, and five-star spice
mixing ingredients well
Increase heat to high, adding water and soy sauce
Cover and steam quickly until cabbage is wilted.
Serve immediately! Bon-appetite!

LASHAWN'S BUTTER BEANS WITH HAM HOCKS

Ingredients:
3 large ham hocks
3 cups of water
1 ½ lb. of fresh butter beans
1 tablespoon of sugar
½ lb. of cut okra
1 ½ teaspoon of salt
1 teaspoon of black pepper

Directions:
Boil ham hocks in a large pot for 20 minutes, reduce heat and bring to simmer for
25 more minutes
Remove ham hocks and cut meat from the bone
into pieces or shredded
Return hock pieces to the pot and add beans. Turn heat
to simmer state
Stir in remaining ingredients and simmer for additional
25 minutes or until beans and okra are tender
Serve!

MERCY'S SIMPLE COUNTRY POTATO SALAD
Ingredients:
6 medium-sized potatoes, peeled, cubed, and cooked
2 large ribs of celery, diced
1 medium-sized onion, diced
3 hard-boiled eggs, diced
½ teaspoon of salt
1 cup of mayonnaise or salad dressing

Directions:
Combine potatoes, celery, onions, and eggs
Sprinkle with salt
Stir in mayonnaise or salad dressing
Chill and serve

BRENDA'S TASTE TOO GOOD! TUNA SALAD

Ingredients:
6 ounce can of tuna
1 ½ cups of diced celery
3 hard-boiled eggs, diced
2 tablespoons minced onions
¼ teaspoon salt
¼ teaspoon pepper
½ cup of mayonnaise, or salad dressing
Lettuce leaves, bread, or sandwich rolls

Directions:
Combine all ingredients, except lettuce, bread, and rolls
mixing lightly
Chill… Serve as a salad or as a sandwich filling

STEPHANIE'S
SUNNY DELIGHT CHICKEN SALAD

Ingredients:
Two 10 oz. cans of chicken salad
One bottle of Hidden Valley Salad Dressing
One packet of Hidden Valley Seasonal Mix (Powder)

Directions:
Pour both cans of chicken into a bowl
Separate the chicken chunks with a
fork
Add 2 tablespoons of seasonal mix
Pour 1 cup of salad dressing
Mix well together and serve

SIMONE'S SASSY SEAFOOD SALAD!

Ingredients:

½ lb. dry elbow macaroni, cooked and drained
½ lb. cooked shrimp, cut into pieces
½ lb. imitation crab meat, cut into pieces
1 cup of mayonnaise
1 teaspoon of ground mustard
1 tablespoon of ketchup
1 tablespoon of sugar
½ cup of celery, chopped fine
¼ cup of green pepper, chopped fine
Salt to taste
Pepper to taste
Lawry seasoning to taste
Garlic powder to taste
Dash of Paprika
Dash of crush red pepper

Directions:

Combine all ingredients except paprika
Mix well and pour into a serving bowl
Sprinkle with paprika. Chill...

TAMMY'S MACARONI SALAD

Ingredients:

8-oz. package dry elbow macaroni
1 tablespoon of salt
3 quarts of water
½ cup of chopped salary
¼ cup of diced green pepper
¾ cup of mayonnaise or salad dressing
2 tablespoons of prepared mustard
¼ teaspoon of onion salt
Dash of Accent

Directions:

Cook macaroni in 3 quarts of salted boiling water
For 10 minutes. Rinse with cold water and drain
Combine all ingredients and toss lightly
Chill for several hours

VINCENT'S FAMOUS CORN PUDDING

Ingredients:

1/2 cup butter
1/2 cup of sugar
2 large eggs
1 cup sour cream
1 package of cornbread muffin mix
½ cup of milk
1 can of whole kernel corn
1 can cream-styled corn

Directions:

Pre-heat oven 350-degrees
Simply combine all ingredients in a bowl and stir well
Pour mixture into cooking pan smoothing out any lumps
Bake in the oven for 45 minutes

DESSERTS
BREAD
ETC

JUANITA'S PEACH COBBLER

Ingredients:
2 cans of Sliced Peaches
2 sticks of butter (chopped into slices)
2 tsp. Lemon extract
2 tsp. Vanilla Flavor
2 cups of sugar
2 cups of self-rising flour
16 Ounces of Water
Crisco Lard (shortening)

Directions:
Pour peaches into the cooking pan and add sugar, lemon extract, and vanilla flavor. Add chopped slices of butter and stir well.
Pour flour into a bowl with two heaping (large spoons) of Crisco Lard, gradually adding water to make doughy. Roll dough on wax paper, kneading dough on cooking sheet. Sprinkle flour on dough again, cutting into strips. Lay strips across the top of the mixture and place them into the oven in a 350-degree oven. Bake for 15 minutes, remove from oven and cut moderately cooked dough into the mix. Cut more strips of dough lying across the top layer of the cobbler. Bake for
15 minutes remove from oven and sprinkle sugar on top of strips of dough. Bake for 15 minutes or until golden brown.

EBONY JOCIE-MAE'S EXCLUSIVE POUND CAKE

Ingredients:
5 eggs
3 sticks of Real Butter
3 cups sugar
3 cups All-purpose Flour
1 cup of milk
4 ounces of sour cream
1/2 Teaspoon Baking Powder
1/2 Teaspoon Salt
2 Teaspoon Vanilla Flavor

Directions:
Step One:

Preheat the Oven to 325 degrees. Grease and flour Bundt Pan

Step Two:
Place sugar and butter in a large mixing bowl. Cream together using a mixer. Add eggs one at a time, beating for 45 seconds after each addition. Next, add vanilla extract and sour cream and beat for 30 seconds

Step Three:
Combine flour,baking powder, and salt in a bowl
Add 1/2 of the dry ingredients to the butter and egg mixture; mixing on low speed until blended
Add 1/2 cup milk and beat on low speed until blended
Repeat with remaining dry ingredients and milk.

Step Four:
 Pour batter into the prepared baking pan, filling no more than 2/3 full. Smooth the top with a spoon or a spatula

Step Five:
Bake in the pre-heated oven until a toothpick inserted into the center comes out clean, and the cake is just starting to pull away from the sides of the pan, about 1 hour and 10 minutes. Remove from the oven and allow to cool for about 15 minutes before inverting onto a plate

AUNT VERA'S CREAM CHEESECAKE

Ingredients:

3 sticks Parkay margarine
1 8oz. package of Philly's Cream Cheese
3 cups sugar
6 eggs x-large
1 tsp vanilla extract
1 tsp lemon extract
3 cups sifted (Swan cake) flour
Add a pinch of salt to flour in the sifter

Directions:

Cream Parkay and cream cheese well
Add sugar and cream after each cup is added
Add eggs one at a time, mixing after each egg
Add vanilla extract and mix well
Add lemon extract and mix well
Add flour one cup at a time, mix well after each cup is added
Grease Bundt pan and bake at 350-degrees for 1 ½ hour
(DO NOT PREHEAT OVEN)

AUNT VERA'S FRUIT CAKE

Ingredients:
1-pound box brown sugar
1-pound margarine
6 egg yolks beaten
2 cups all-purpose flour
1 teaspoon baking powder
1 2oz. bottle lemon extract
1 quart chopped pecans
½ pound candied pineapple chopped
½ pound candied cherries chopped
6 egg whites beaten

Directions:
Cream together sugar and margarine until smooth; add beaten egg yolks and mix well. Combine 2 cups flour and baking powder, add to cream mixture. Cover and let stand overnight. The next day pour the mixture into a greased Bundt pan and bake at 250 degrees for 2 ½ hours or until done. (DO NOT PREHEAT OVEN)

NYLAH'S SO GOOD! STRAWBERRY LEMON CHEESECAKE

Ingredients:

Salted butter
Sugar
Eggs
Graham Pie Crust
Lemon
Lemon Extract
Vanilla Extract
Cream Cheese
Sour Cream
Fresh Strawberries

For the Cheesecake:

1 Graham Pie Crust
¾ cup granulated sugar or to liking
1 Tbsp packed lemon zest
2 (8 oz) pkgs. cream cheese, softened (I always recommend using Philadelphia for cheesecake)
3 large eggs
¼ cup sour cream
2 Tbsp lemon fresh lemon
1 – 1 ½ tsp lemon extract, to taste
½ tsp vanilla extract

Strawberry Sauce:

8 oz fresh strawberries
2 Tbsp sugar , or to taste
2 tsp fresh lemon juice

Directions:

For the graham pie crust:
Preheat oven to 350 degrees. Bake crust in preheated oven 5 minutes then remove from oven and set aside to cool
Reduce oven temperature to 325 degrees
In a food processor, pulse together ¾ cup granulated sugar
with lemon zest (if you don't have a food processor you can just rub the sugar and lemon zest together with your fingertips)

Add cream cheese to a mixing bowl and pour sugar mixture over cream cheese and using an electric hand mixer set on low speed, blend mixture together just until smooth. Stir in eggs one at a time, mixing just until combined after each addition

Blend in sour cream and heavy cream. Stir in lemon juice, lemon extract and vanilla extract.
Tap mixing bowl against counter-top to release some of the air bubbles, about 30 times
Pouring mixture over crust and fill pie crust up. Bake in preheated oven 20 - 25 minutes until centers only giggle slightly (pie will sink when removed from oven)

Allow to cool to room temperature, about 1 hour, then refrigerate until set, at least 2 hours. Serve with strawberry sauce.
For the Strawberry Sauce:
Add strawberries, 1 Tbsp sugar and 2 tsp lemon juice to a food processor and blend until pureed. Chill in refrigerator until ready to use

LUCY'S CLASSIC CHOCOLATE CAKE

Ingredients:
½ stick of butter
¼ cup. of vegetable oil
2 cups of sugar
1 teaspoon of vanilla
2 eggs
¼ teaspoon of baking soda
1 ¾ cups of flour
¼ teaspoon of baking powder
½ teaspoon of salt
1 ¼ cups of milk

Directions:
Cream together in stand mixer butter, oil, and sugar
Blend in eggs and vanilla
In a separate bowl, stir together dry ingredients
Add mixture to creamed blended mix with milk
Beat well after each addition. Until well combined
Spread butter into 9' square baking dish
Bake at 350-degrees for 30-35 minutes or until inserted
Pick in center of cake comes out clean

KANEESHA'STHREE LAYERCARAMEL CAKE

Ingredients:
FiveCups of sugar
Three sticks of salted butter
Three eggs
Two cups of self-rising flour
Whole milk
Vanilla Extract
1 can of carnation milk
Baker's Joy baking spray

Directions:
Preheat oven on 350
In a mixing bowl add two cups of sugar, two sticks of butter
Blend well
Add eggs one at a time
Add flower and slowly add milk until desired consistency
Add one table spoon of vanilla extract
Mix well
Spray pans with baker's joy
Equally divide batter into pans
Bake until done test by sticking a tooth pick in cake (if it comes out clean its done)

Caramel Icing:
In a saucepan add one stick of butter, carnation milk, one teaspoon vanilla extract, and three cups of sugar
Cook on low until it bubble and thickens
Let cool and spread on cake layers

HATTIE'S SWEET POTATO PIE
Ingredients:
4-6 lbs. medium-sized sweet potatoes
2 sticks of unsalted butter
1 ½ cups of sugar
4-6 eggs
2 tablespoons of flour
½ cup of carnation milk
Ground nutmeg to taste
9'inch unbaked crust

Directions:
Boil potatoes until soft
Peel them and mash to smooth consistency
Add sugar, butter, eggs, and flour mix well
Pour mixture into pie crust
Bake at 350-degrees for 1-1½ hours until
lightly browned & set aside. Cool before slicing

JUDIE'S FRIED APPLES

Ingredients:
4 Apples, preferably greens
2 tablespoons of butter
½ cup of brown sugar
2 tablespoons of water

Directions:
Core apples and cut into circles
Sauté' in butter turning often until soft but still
holding their shape
Stir in brown sugar and water
Continue cooking until apples are coated with syrup

JANET'S SUGAR COOKIES

Ingredients:
1 ½ Cups of sugar
2 sticks of butter at room temperature
3 eggs
1 teaspoon of baking soda
1 cup of buttermilk
1 teaspoon of vanilla extract
4 ½ cups of flour
2 teaspoons of baking powder

Directions:
Mix well sugar, butter, and eggs
Add baking soda, milk, and vanilla, mix well
Sift together flour and baking powder and add
To mixture and mix well
Drop by teaspoons onto greased cookie sheet
Bake at 400-degrees for 8-10 minutes

ZA'NIYA& CALEAH FAMOUS CHOCOLATE CHIPCOOKIES

Ingredients:
1 cup butter, softened
1 cup white sugar
1 cup packed brown sugar
2 eggs

2 teaspoons vanilla extract
1 teaspoon baking soda
2 teaspoons hot water
½ teaspoon salt
3 cups all-purpose flour

2 cups semisweet chocolate chips

1 cup chopped walnuts

Directions:
Mix all ingredients together well
Drop by teaspoon onto greased cookie sheet
Bake at 375-degrees for 10-15 minutes

WARREN, KABREYAH, AND KEJUAN'S BROWNIE'S

Ingredients:
½ cup butter
1 cup white sugar
2 eggs
1 teaspoon vanilla extract
cup unsweetened cocoa powder
½ cup all-purpose flour
¼ teaspoon salt
¼ teaspoon baking powder

Frosting:
3 tablespoons butter, softened
3 tablespoons unsweetened cocoa powder
1 tablespoon honey
1 teaspoon vanilla extract
1 cup confectioners' sugar

Directions:
Preheat oven to 350 degrees F (175 degrees C). Grease and flour an 8-inch square pan.In a large saucepan, melt 1/2 cup butter. Remove from heat, and stir in sugar, eggs, and 1 teaspoon vanilla. Beat in 1/3 cup cocoa, 1/2 cup flour, salt, and baking powder. Spread batter into prepared pan.Bake in preheated oven for 25 to 30 minutes. Do not overcook.To Make Frosting: Combine 3 tablespoons softened butter, 3 tablespoons cocoa, honey, 1 teaspoon vanilla extract, and 1 cup confectioners' sugar. Stir until smooth. Frost brownies while they are still warm

JAYLA'S WONDERFUL WAFFLES
Ingredients:
2 eggs
2 cups of all-purpose flour
½ cup of vegetable oil
1 tablespoon of white sugar
4 teaspoons of baking powder
¼ teaspoon of salt
½ teaspoon of vanilla extract

Directions:

Preheat waffle iron
Beat eggs in large bowl with hand beater until fluffy
Beat in flour, milk, vegetable oil, sugar, baking powder,
salt, and vanilla util smooth
Spray preheated waffle iron with non-stick cooking spray
Pour mix onto hot waffle iron
Cook until golden brown
Serve hot!

Optional: Spray with whip cream in a circular rotation on top
Of waffles. Add strawberry slices and sprinkle cinnamon on top for preferred
taste

IT'S YUMMY FOR YOUR TUMMY!

"THE REAL" KIM MEXICAN CORNBREAD

Ingredients:

Onion (chopped)
Bell pepper (chopped)
Can on Mexican corn
Three boxes of Jiffy cornbread
5 lbs. of ground beef
Lawry seasoning salt
Garlic powder

Directions:

Brown ground beef, mix onions, and bell peppers, then drain fat from the
mixture; after you drain it, put it back in the pot and return to the stove. Add
corn and seasoning to the pot and let it simmer for about 10 minutes; set aside

Make up your cornbread mix using directions on the box and set-in casserole
dish, pour the ground beef mixture into the container, smoothing it out. Pour
cornbread on top of ground beef, mix and spread evenly. Bake until cornbread
is done, and let the dish stand for 20-25 minutes
Serve!

AUNTY V'S HOT WATER CORNBREAD

Ingredients:

Hot Water Cornbread
"Hot Rize" corn meal
Sugar
Water
Vegetable oil

Directions:

Mix 1 cup of cornmeal and a half tablespoon of sugar in a bowl
Add boiling hot water to the mixture
Don't add too much water that it's runny
You want it to be at a consistency to your preference
So, add a little water at a time and mix
Heat on medium high the vegetable oil in a heavy pan,
I prefer cast iron
Form cornbread and fry in the pan
Adjust heat. Brown on both sides
Normally, 1 min per side

JAYLA, BRIANA, KA'MILAH, AND PATRICK JR. FAMOUS STRAWBERRY LEMONADE

Ingredients:

3 scoops of sugar
2 16 Oz. cups of water
1 cup of water (for simple syrup)
1 cup of fresh lemon juice (10 lemons)
3-5 lemons sliced
8-10 strawberries
20 ounces of canned or fresh Pineapples

So, add a little water at a time and mix
Heat on medium high the vegetable oil in a heavy pan,
I prefer cast iron
Form cornbread and fry in the pan
Adjust heat. Brown on both sides
Normally, 1 min per side

Directions:

Step 1: Make a simple syrup by heating the sugar and 1 cup of water
With fruit in a small sauce-pan until sugar dissolves completely

Vegetable oil

Step 2: While sugar is dissolving, mash the fruit to create a syrup

Step 3: Juice the lemons (squeeze) and drain fruit syrup with lemon
Juice to a container. Add 2-3 (16 ounces) of cold water more or less
To desired strength) and refrigerate

Step 4: Taste for sweetness and add strawberries, pineapples and
Lemon slices. Stir or shake briskly, depending on the container Refrigerate and
once cold, serve!

YUMMY!

ISAIAH & BINK'S PARTYDON'T STOP ICEY PUNCH!

Ingredients:

6 cups of orange juice
2 cup of fresh sliced strawberries
1 quart of apple juice
1 quart of Sunkist orange soda
1 quart of ginger ale
2 cups of cranberry juice
2 cups of pineapple juice
½ cup of sugar

Directions:

Combine 3 cups of orange juice and strawberries
Freeze in a container to make larger ice cubes
Chill apple juice, orange soda, ginger ale, cranberry juice,
pineapple juice, and 3 cups of orange juice, and sugar, stir well
Combine chilled ingredients in the punch bowl
Add orange juice-strawberry ice cubes

DELICIOUS!!!!

JADA'S BANANA BREAD

Ingredients:
3 ripe bananas, mashed
1 cup of white sugar
1 egg
¼ cup of melted butter
1 ½ cup of all- purpose flour
1 teaspoon of baking soda
1 teaspoon of salt

Directions:
Preheat oven on 350 degrees
Combine all ingredients in bowl mix well
Pour into non-stick pan
Cook for 60-65 minutes

JAMES SIMPLE CHOCOLATE PUDDING RECIPE

Ingredients:
1 cup of sugar
1/2 cup of baking cocoa
1/4 cup of corn starch
1/2 teaspoon of salt
4 cups of whole milk
2 tablespoons of softened butter
2 teaspoons of vanilla extract

Directions:
In a medium saucepan combine all ingredients and
add ½ teaspoon of salt
Boil mixture on mild to moderate heat (medium)
Incorporate pudding into 6-ounce ramekins and refrigerate until chilled

JURNEE'S JOLLY RANCHER JELLO

Ingredients:
3 oz. of water
1 cup of boiling water
1 bag of hard Jolly Ranchers
2 oz. small plastic cups
Non-stick spray

Directions:
Add 1 cup of boiling water to mixture
Stir until completely dissolved (about 2 minutes)
Add one cup of cold water
Place mixture in desired containers
Place mixture in refrigerator 60-90 minutes

CARNELL IV' "KING"SNOW CONE TOPPING

Ingredients:
2 cups of white sugar
1 cup of water
1 (0.13 ounce) package of unsweetened
  fruit flavored soft drink mix (I love cherry!)

Directions:
In a sauce pan stir the sugar and water
Bring to a boil for about 1 minute
Remove from heat and stir in drink mix
Allow to cool and store in a container for pouring
Pour over shaved ice and serve

www.ingramcontent.com/pod-product-compliance
Lightning Source LLC
LaVergne TN
LVHW070013090426
835508LV00048B/3391